Facilitating Corporate Solutions

ACTIVITIES TO TEACH SOFT SKILLS

AS FACILITATED BY DARIN PHILLIPS

ISBN 1-59113-170-7

Published by Darin Phillips, USA.

PRINTED IN THE UNITED STATES OF AMERICA

Booklocker.com, Inc.
2003

http://www.darinphillips.com/home.htm
darin@darinphillips.com

Facilitating Corporate Solutions

ACTIVITIES TO TEACH SOFT SKILLS

AS FACILITATED BY DARIN PHILLIPS

WARNING

The activities in this book are intended only for use by trained facilitators of experiential activities. By choosing to facilitate the activities herein, the facilitator assumes all responsibility and liability for any and all situations which may arise as a result of utilizing the activities and releases the publisher, author, their heirs, staff, and associates from any and all liability.

Table of Contents

Introduction

Adults learn best when the trainer values the information already present in the student's head. With soft skills, this is particularly true. Most classes redundantly repeat what your grandmother and mom already told you.

During the ten years that I spent as a counselor prior to joining the ranks of the world's consultants and trainers, I learned that people value their own solutions. When someone uses 'your' solution it will not work and you are the one to blame. If someone uses 'their' solution they own the outcome and will make sure the idea works.

These classic therapeutic activities are meant to be facilitated, not trained. This allows the learner to define the outcomes, but by their very nature, the outcomes are guided by the trainer's presentation and questions. This model facilitates ownership and buy-in by your trainees.

The exercises that you will find in '*Facilitating Corporate Solutions*' have been modified and scripted to meet the needs of corporate groups. These presentations have been utilized by the author over 500 times each. The scripts should be modified to fit your preferred presentation style and the industry of your client group. The limits of these activities are truly controlled only by the creativity of the facilitator.

Activity

1

Pass the Client

Here is an opportunity to discuss the balance between quality and efficiency in handling internal and external customer requests.

This activity is extremely fun if you take the time to collect interesting soft balls for your 'bag of tricks'. Safe items to throw that are also humorous include squeaky pet toys, balls with faces, small stuffed animals, and beanbags that talk when dropped. These items can represent customers, stakeholders, vendors, supervisors, direct reports, or even the members of the group you are facilitating.

EQUIPMENT

▪ Bag with at least 20 soft balls
▪ Stopwatch
▪ Flipchart
▪ Markers

Be sure to stop the group if they begin to throw the objects 'at' each other instead of 'to' each other.

Never use sharp or heavy items in your bag of tricks.

Presentation

Ask one team member to volunteer to be the first person that a client will come into contact within this team. Hand that person one ball and announce that this is a client. If it is a funny ball, then you may also comment that they may recognize this client.

> **Technique** You might want to have the group select four or five criteria in addition to 'no drops' to define customer satisfaction. Write those on the flipchart to review after each attempt..

Now explain, "All clients must begin and end with ____________ (volunteer's name). The clients want to meet every member of the team once before deciding whether to work with this team or not. That means that the client must pass from one team member to another until everyone has had direct contact with the client before it comes back to ____________ (the volunteer). If you have not yet received the client, please hold both hands out in front of you to show that you are ready. Oh, and initially, please do not pass the client to the person directly to your right or left... just for this first time, and also please remember who you are passing the client to because you must keep all subsequent clients in the same order as your first one. You may begin."

They may ask you questions and some clarification may be made, but do not repeat the instructions more than twice. One or more of the group members then should know the answer.

"Okay, was this customer satisfied? Are they going to give your team their business? Did you treat them the way you treat potential clients?" If the ball was dropped, then the customer was definitely not satisfied.

"It is time to bring up 'consensus'. You must decide on a goal, as a team, of how many customers that you may successfully introduce to the team using this order. Consensus does not necessarily mean that any individual is more right than another (we all know that our idea is the best idea after all), but rather that everyone give 100% effort to the best idea or goal for the team whether it is the best idea for them personally or not. So you have one minute to set a goal for the number of clients that you may successfully meet using the order you made in the first pass." They will also be timed, but do not bring that up yet.

"So who believes that this team can handle *x* number of clients?" Empower any dissenters to share their concerns and work toward consensus.

Hand the volunteer the number of balls that the team chose. The volunteer must begin and end with all of the clients so they may seek a resource to hold them with.

"Are you ready? On your mark, get set, GROW!" At this point begin timing the team with a stopwatch. Differences in the end may come down to tenths or hundredths of a second.

"Okay, are all of the clients satisfied? That took this team *x* minute(s) and *y* seconds. Of course that means that you have established a benchmark. Oh, and I have also received this memo from the corporate office/board of directors/company president. (Rattle a piece of paper.) It reads, 'Congratulations on an excellent effort in attracting clients to our services and products. Because of your commitment and dedication we have met our goals for the month. However, please be advised that in order to meet our next month's goal, your team must successfully pass the same number of customers in x seconds. Thank you very much for your attention to this matter, etc., etc.' You have two minutes to problem-solve, plan and practice before trying the next month's pass." Field any questions. Remind the group that they are empowered to see the opportunities instead of the restrictions if they ask questions about what can be done or you may say, "Does that meet the guidelines given?"

"It is time to begin, are you ready? On your mark, get set, GROW!" Time them again.

If customers drop or the time is not met allow another planning time. If they make it, get a feel for the group and if it is appropriate challenge them further. "You have met their expectations, but is that the best time for this team? What sorts of rewards or incentives could be had for exceeding expectations?"

Allow the team to repeat until they reach the most excitement for being successful as possible. If they are not celebrating their success, point that out. Many companies have gotten away form celebrating and instead only notice when expectations are not met, is this one of those? How does this team want to react to success?

Collect your balls and have them get in a circle where everyone is shoulder-to-shoulder or so that there is only one level. It is important that everyone can easily see everyone else, which facilitates communication in large groups. Begin processing.

Debrief

The following questions can spark performance-focused discussion:

- What was different between the initial attempt and the final one?
- How are customers really treated by this team? How do you want to treat them? What will you do differently starting now?
- How did the team decide to balance quality and speed? If you were the customer, which would you value most?

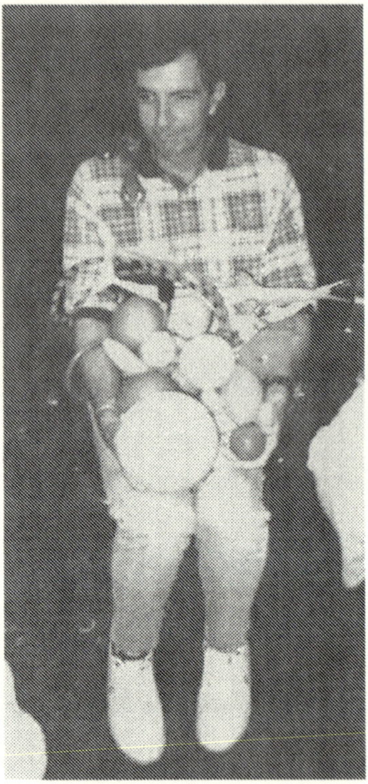

FIGURE 1

The person who volunteers to have first and last contact with the clients often ends up with more than they bargained for!

Corporate Raiders

Activity 2

This activity provides your group with an 'AHA!' - competition can be a destructive and frustrating alternative to collaboration.

Try to think of a resource that your group truly competes for. In a grocery store this might be shelf space, in a sales department this might be hot leads, or in an eCommerce company this might be search engine ranking. Though everyone benefits from the success of other teammates, the mindset begins with an assumption of a win-lose outcome.

EQUIPMENT

▪ Bag with at least 60 soft balls
▪ 3 Hula Hoops
▪ Flipchart
▪ Markers

Be sure to stop the group if they run, try to tackle or hurt each other, or if they throw the objects.

Presentation

Place all of the balls and objects into the hoop in the center of the playing field.

Place one hoop for each sub-group that you will divide the team into equidistant from the center and each other. If there are three sub-groups, then you will have a triangle with a hoop full of balls in the center.

Technique Start the activity quickly with, "On your mark, get set, go!" to encourage the assumption of competition.

Divide the team and have each division go to a hoop.

"The objects in the center of the team are potential clients / sales / bonuses. The objective is for the team to get all of the objects into one hoop. You may take objects from the center hoop or from another hoop (gesture to the sub-group's hoops). In the first minute of the activity, you may only touch one object. In the second minute you may only touch two objects, and on and on. I will call out when you may begin to carry more. You may not touch any other participants, you may only walk fast, there is no running allowed, and you may not throw the objects - they must remain in someone's hand or on the ground inside a hoop. Again, No running, No throwing, No touching, and you may get objects from anyone's hoop. GO!!!!!!" You will want to call the object by its name for this game instead of using the word object each time, which increases their desire to have it. Be prepared for some serious competition instead of cooperation at first. There is no rule against moving the hoops. I usually call out, "You may now carry two/three/etc. objects," every thirty to forty seconds to speed up the activity. One full minute is a long time.

Have the team circle up after all of the balls are placed into one hoop (are there holdouts?). Make sure the circle is one-person deep so that everyone may be seen and heard. Process the activity by asking, "What happened?" and "So what did you learn from all of this?" Point out that the activities that the team (it is still just *one team*, even if artificially divided) will encounter throughout the day will require that they work together, not competing against anyone but himself or herself to be the best team possible. That is the key to success on the course.

Debrief

Questions that make the point:

- What does win-lose look like and feel like?
- How does a win-win solution feel different?
- Where do you experience destructive competition at work? Constructive competition?

FIGURE 2

Everyone is thinking, "Hurry up and finish the stupid instructions! I want that really big ball."

Activity

3

The Corporate Game

It is uncomfortable, they don't like it, but they have ALWAYS done it that way...

When you want to make the point that innovative, out of the box thinking can create more effective and efficient solutions, this activity will drive the point home. The team begins in an awkward and uncomfortable position and will initially assume that they must remain in that position until the activity is complete. They may even chastise the person that suggests that the team should get out of the corporate position.

EQUIPMENT

▪ 2 Hula Hoops
▪ Stopwatch
▪ Flipchart
▪ Markers

Lower back problems can be accommodated by putting those people at the end of the line, holding the next person's hand, but not bent over in the corporate position.

Presentation

Have the participants line up in a single-file line by number of days with their company.

"Who knows 'the corporate position'?" You may have responses about the position that their company is taking on some stand, but look for someone to bend over and then recognize them for knowing, "Ah, I see _______ knows the corporate position! Would you please share that with the group?" If no one bends over or describes bending over, ask, "What does it mean at your office to 'assume the position'?" This is more direct and always elicits at least one correct answer to work with.

> **Technique** Slowly pull a sheet of paper from your pocket and announce that you have received a pocket fax from the President of the company who is challenging the team to cut their time in half.

"Well, that is very close. Actually, the corporate position is (demonstrate while describing) knees bent, right hand forward and left hand back between your knees. Let's all try the corporate position now... knees bent, right hand forward, left hand back... Very good!"

"Now does anyone have a back problem? If so, please take care of yourself by moving to one end of the line." The back of the line is best and if several people have back problems ask them to do the position without the left hand going between their knees, just to the person next to them.

"I would like everyone to make a left (or right) face. (Everyone should be facing the back of the person in front of him or her.) Please assume the corporate position. You will find that there is hand in front of you to shake with your right hand. Please hold that hand." Give Hula-Hoops to the participants at each end of the line.

"Here are your guidelines:

Number One - you must begin in the corporate position,

Number Two - you must remain in contact with each other until the task is complete, contact being holding each other's hands,

Number Three - the task is complete when everyone has passed through both hoops, the hoop in front ends up with _____________ (the person in the rear), and the hoop in back ends up with _______________ (the person in the front).

One safety concern to mention. There is no biting allowed. Persons biting the hoops have injured the teammate in front of them before. You may begin!" They have been connected in the corporate position through all three guidelines so there may be considerable confusion and discomfort. One end will try something without the other end knowing and there may be blame and lack of communication between participants. Different interpretations of the guidelines will be evident and the facilitator may ask, "What did the team hear?" Time this first attempt and announce the time to the group when they are done. Also, did anyone break contact?

"Is that the best time that this team can achieve?" Many tired persons will respond, "YES!!!", but the team will decide that they can beat that time. Ask them to set a goal or let them attempt to get a 'best' time.

"You have two minutes to brainstorm and problem-solve this activity." Repeat the guidelines no more than twice and then ask the team what they heard/understood/etc.

Loudly announce the time and allow brainstorming time again after each attempt until the celebration or your best judgment indicates that the best time has been reached. Persons with back problems should be encouraged to not bend over after successive attempts. If the team does not identify that they can get out of the corporate position (isn't it more comfortable?), or that the persons on the end can use their free hand to guide the hoops, or that they do not have to end in the corporate position, then announce that an idea or resource has not been fully utilized. Normally, they will want to find out what this is.

Debrief

Recommended questions:

- Why did the team want to give up before reaching peak performance?
- What had to happen to make you realize your own potential?
- Where do you have systems and processes at work that unnecessarily burden employees? What can you do to repair them?

FIGURE 3

When the hoops cross each other life gets a little more interesting.

Activity

4

Two-Minute Beetle Tag

Between sessions you can warm up the troops in a fun and energizing way.

Have you ever wondered what it would be like to live in a terrarium? Your group will become a bunch of insects inside the terrarium that was formerly known as a conference room.

EQUIPMENT

- A conference room or orange cones to mark four corners of the terrarium

No running is allowed because everyone must touch heel-to-toe.

Presentation

Mark a restrictive boundary and explain that everyone will need a partner and to please step with their partner into the terrarium. The terrarium has glass walls identified by the cones.

"You are all beetles, the insect, not the rock group. And as beetles, this is how you move... the only way that you may move during this activity." Walk heel-to-toe around the group. Make sure you touch your heel and toe on each step.

"Please decide who will be the first chaser between you and your partner because this is a tag game. The chaser only chases their partner, but at the same time a lot of other beetles are scampering around inside this terrarium." After they have decided who will chase whom, announce, "If the person being chased is tagged, then they must turn in a circle three times with one hand up in the air before they may begin chasing their partner." Demonstrate this.

"As one last reminder, tagging your partner, as you may remember from grade school, is only to be done with an open hand, gently to the back between the shoulders and hips. Please do not slap or hit anyone." Demonstrate.

"The game will begin when I have finished counting to five. All beetles may not move if they are the chasers as I count so that their partners have a head start to get away. Ready? One... two..."

At the conclusion of the activity ask, "Why do you think we played this game?" The two real purposes are to get people to laugh ("What did you hear a lot of?") and to get their blood flowing again (it is a good activity after lunch). Point out that it is an excellent game because no one had any special advantage over his or her partner unless there was a huge difference in shoe size.

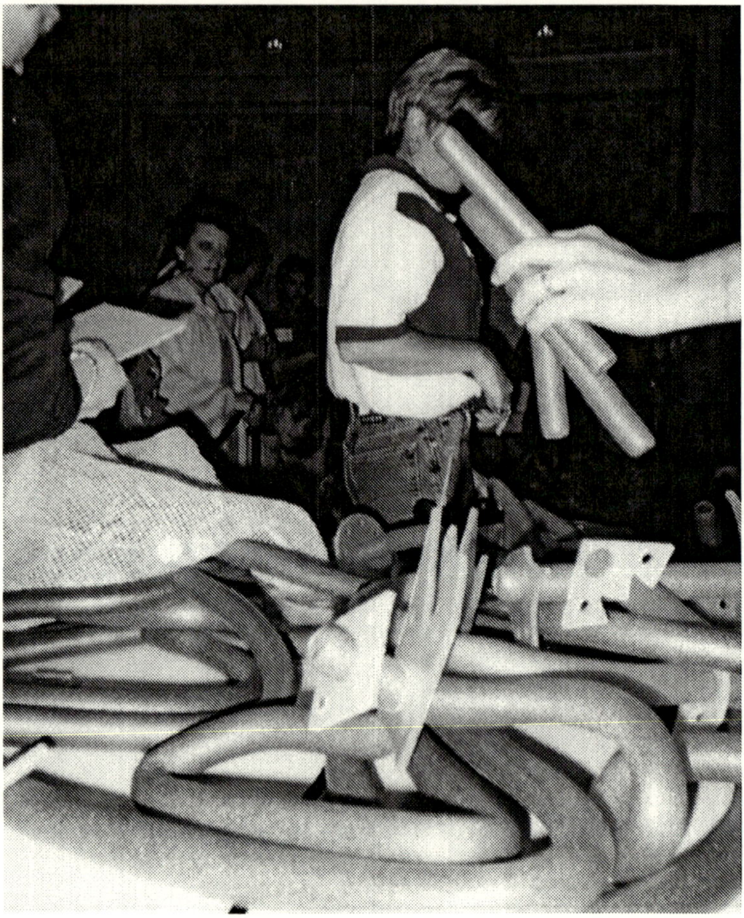

FIGURE 4

Allow your group to Beetle-ize with fun accessories to wear.

Activity 5

Creating a Shared Vision

Your organization has just announced a new vision statement - an isosceles triangle.

Many organizations announce a new vision, mission, or values statement and expect the employees to begin to live that statement immediately. However, what happens when everyone knows the words of the vision and interpret it differently? This activity will show the group what might happen.

EQUIPMENT

▪ 25-foot rope tied into a giant circle
▪ Flipchart
▪ Markers

Remove or stand in front of hazards such as tables, trees, extension cords, and holes.

Presentation

"Here we have your computer network (hold up the rope). I need everyone to get on-line. That means hold onto this rope with both hands. You may slide up and down the rope, but you may not let go of the rope with either hand. Now to simulate being in your respective offices, please close your eyes so that you may not see each other. You may communicate verbally, i.e. through e-mail, but you must resist the temptation to peek at your teammates. The task assigned to this team is to form the network, the rope, into an isosceles triangle while standing and then set it on the ground. You may begin." Now someone or several someone's must take charge or problem-solve this, beginning with the definition of an isosceles triangle. Watch the dynamics closely for useful information to use during processing. Perhaps write the most poignant or prescriptive quotes that you hear (without naming names) on the flipchart. Try to recognize during processing the persons who used clear communication, had good ideas, showed excellent leadership qualities, or persons who had the most integrity by not peeking.

If the team is not satisfied with the triangle they end up with, they can choose to try again. It may help to allow a face-to-face planning session prior to starting again. What did this teach the team? What would they like to carry over to the office from this activity? Where do communication barriers such as these (at work) challenge them? How would those be successfully overcome now? Write all of the answers on the flipchart - this is the real learning that can be applied back at work.

> **Technique** Many shapes can be formed with the rope, but the facilitator must use a very specific shape. If you say 'star', they may create an outline of Bruce Willis' face.

Now they may try a more complex task using the full vision that they may have discovered is necessary.

"Everyone please take the rope in your hands again. This time you are in a meeting together, face-to-face so you do not need to close your eyes. Without letting go of the rope with either hand (your hands may slide back and forth), please form a five-pointed star that crosses in five places such as the ones you used to draw in grade school." Be prepared to draw it on the ground or have a picture prepared to show them a star. How was the experience different this time? Why? What do you want to take back to the office from this?

Debrief

Cause the group to think about the outcomes:

- What is required to make sure everyone will leave this meeting sharing the same information with his or her coworkers?

- What are the elements of effective communication as you experienced them?

- Where can you look for ideas and solutions at your company?

FIGURE 5

A fun variation allows your participants to be inside a large Bungee loop to form their shape.

Activity

6

Diminishing Resources

If you are asking your group to do more with less, this activity is for you.

Assumptions limit organizations by creating artificial barriers. If you want your team to become possibility thinkers, this activity will help them break out of that box. You may consider the effects that this will have right before your participants begin a strategic planning session.

EQUIPMENT

▪ One carpet square, plastic pad, or paper plate per participant
▪ Masking tape on every pad for writing
▪ Ball point pens

Clear the area of hazards such as pins in the carpet, chairs and tables, or sticks.

Presentation

"I would like everyone to please take a carpet square and label it with the name of the greatest resource you have in your office. The one thing you rely so heavily on that you could never live without it." Give out the pens and give them time to think and write. When they are done have them form a large circle.

> **Technique** Listen very carefully for the first person that mentions the ultimate solution so you can call on them during the discussion that follows the activity.

"Okay, one-at-a-time, please announce to the team what your resource is and then lay it out in the middle of the circle somewhere, you will be able to move them wherever you want inside the circle before you begin." Allow them to call out the resource and lay down the carpet square. If they were quiet or soft-spoken, repeat their resource name loudly such as by saying, "Okay, Jean says her resource is the telephone!"

"Now the task is really quite simple. You must do three things: Number One - You must all be connected physically, Number Two - You must all be off of the ground for, Number Three - The count of three. So you must remain connected and off the ground for the count of three. (Raise a finger as you say each condition.) By off the ground, I mean that no art of you or your clothing may be touching the ground. The only resources you have are the carpet squares and each other to stay off the ground. So for example, this would be off the ground... (Stand on a carpet square.) Any questions?" If they ask what the three things are again ask the group to tell you, raising a finger after each one. If they are wrong, ask them to listen closely and repeat the guidelines only one more time. They may believe that they heard you say, "For three Seconds," but you said, "For the Count of three."

"Please begin." They will classically try to all hold hands standing on the carpet squares and then count, "One, two, three!"

Now you will be bad economic times, or company cutbacks, or broken equipment, or a new policy to do more with less, or the competition luring away staff, etc. Each time you will be something new and you will take 20% of the carpet squares away. For example, if you were the competition, pick up the carpet squares that are actual people, if you are broken equipment, pick up computers, phones, manufacturing equipment, etc., Only take about 20% of the resources the first four times. You will announce, "You have lost use of these resources, but your task remains the same!" If they take a great deal of time, impose a time limit such as, "You have 30 seconds to meet the three conditions!"

On the fifth time, pick up all but one or two carpet squares. Leave these for persons who are not able to jump so that they may participate. The ultimate solution, which the team may reach well before the fifth round anticipating the climax, is to have everyone hold hands and jump simultaneously while some fast talker yells, “Onetwothree!”

The point? No matter what problems arise to cutback on resources, all you really need are each other to get the job done! Brings a tear to your eye, doesn’t it?

Debrief

To foster a quick discussion of the lessons learned:

- How early in the process did the final solution come out? Why did it take so long to implement?
- Why does your organization hold onto solutions even as they become harder to implement?
- What was the most important resource? (The people on the team.)

FIGURE 6

As the resources disappear the team starts to 'feel the love'.

Activity 7

Corporate Sharks

Is your company picked apart by headhunters or recruiters?

If you want to make a statement about protecting resources this activity will enhance the value of any resource in the minds of the team members. The metaphor of protecting valuable employees from headhunters or competitors in your industry works particularly well.

EQUIPMENT

▪ One carpet square, plastic pad, or paper plate per participant	▪ Ball point pens
▪ Masking tape on every pad for writing	▪ Orange cones to mark the start and end
	▪ Bandanna for the facilitator's face
	▪ Flipchart
	▪ Markers

Do not hit or get hit by the team members as you attempt to snatch the resources.

Presentation

If you do not plan to do Diminishing Resources, then I suggest using the tape and labeling the carpet squares as resources. If you have done Diminishing Resources, then ask the team to announce something meaningful. For each thing they can name, they will get a carpet square, but no more than noted in the equipment section. Significant issues to name may have come up for your use, but if not, have them name traits of excellent leadership **or** products in their line that they would like to capitalize on the market with **or** new, untapped markets **or** anything that they would hold in high value. This activity is great for creating a sense of value in something that is perhaps not as valued as it should be by the participants (e.g. administrative staff, managers). No matter what they name, write each one up on the flipchart.

Mark boundaries for a start and finish line at least three feet long for each carpet square that the team has or map out a course that is four feet long for every square.

"These resources/traits/products/markets are extremely valuable commodities and in the business world, when you do not adequately protect your assets, corporate sharks are bound to snatch them up for rival companies. If at any time you do not use one of the squares, a corporate shark will take it. The object is to get from the start to the end of this 'project' without touching the ground. Only your squares may touch the ground. If at any point a team member touches the ground, the team will have the opportunity to try again from the beginning with whatever resources remain at that point. Again, to clarify, you must make it through the 'project', from start to finish, but only the carpet squares may touch the ground. If at any time a square goes unused, it will be taken away and if at any time a team member touches the ground the team will start over. Any questions? You may begin..." You may wish to tie a bandanna around your face like a bandit from the old west as you will quickly snatch any squares that are not being touched constantly by a team member between the start and finish lines. For example, if the team member in front sets a square down and lets go before a foot is on the square, it is not being used for a brief moment and is lost to the corporate sharks. In addition, if someone takes their foot off a square somewhere in the middle of the line before the person behind them puts their foot down, snatch it quickly. The team will quickly protect their squares with great ferocity. They may even attempt to steal them back from you - I allow that. Spot the participants very closely when they have to share resources. It is best that they are reminded to step off and suffer the consequence of starting over than to get actually hurt or to hurt their teammates by pulling several people down with them.

Technique At the end of the path most of the participants will be so excited to finish that they will jump off of the resources, leaving them exposed and vulnerable to your stealing.

In processing the event, you should ask about how these resources/traits/whatever-they-labeled are truly treated and valued by the company. Are they protected as much in reality? Why or why not? Are they truly valuable? Do they make or break the success of projects? How should they be treated in the future?

Debrief

How you can stimulate thinking:

- Whom did the facilitator represent? Who is always trying to take your resources?
- How did the collective attitude toward the facilitator affect the outcome?
- Can you afford to abandon or lose resources at any time, especially toward the end of a project? Why might the team lose focus in the end and what can you do about that at work?

FIGURE 7

As the carpet squares begin to disappear the team will really support each other to guarantee everyone's success.

Activity 8

Emerging Markets

Tag is still one of the best games of all time.

Sales persons are always ambitious and aggressive. Tag is a super way to inspire and promote that competitive fire. This activity will get everyone's blood flowing and point out that strategy is still the best way to capture and maintain market share.

EQUIPMENT

▪ Small bean bag
▪ Two large foam balls
▪ Flipchart
▪ Markers

No one may be hit in the face and those persons trying to snatch the ball should not hit back.

Presentation

One person is asked to volunteer.

"You have discovered a new market, represented by this bean bag. (Drop the bean bag on the ground.) It is still a fragile, emerging market, but everyone wants a piece of it. You will lose this market if you touch it. Meanwhile, your competition is interested in exploiting this market and will stop at nothing to get it, they would even go so far as to touch it in order to take it from you. Your only defenses are two marketing strategies that will freeze the competition in their tracks if you touch them. (Hand the volunteer the foam balls.) The competition is only frozen for the remainder of the activity if the foam balls touch them. Please be aware of the safety concerns associated with tagging someone too fiercely, thank you."

> **Technique** Adding extra bean bags makes the market harder to protect if one person begins to dominate the game.

The volunteer is left to guard their beanbag on the ground.

Tell the rest of the participants, "As a team, your objective is to take this emerging market away from the competition, as represented by ___________ (the volunteer's name). If you are touched by the marketing strategies, you are frozen immediately in whatever position you were in when touched. Whichever team member successfully takes the emerging market away from ____________ will get a very lucrative commission and will get to control that market next. A fully protected territory! Some things to keep in mind: you may not intentionally touch the marketing strategies (foam balls) or _______________ and there should be no running, jumping or diving. You may begin."

Process the competition between the team members trying to get the market or the cooperation they use. How did they view their teammate in the middle? Were they all treated alike? Why? Who was able to get in the middle the most often? What did they do to get that protected territory?

Debrief

Get the team thinking strategically:

- How long did it take the team to start planning together?
- What methods worked best to get the market from the individual?
- How many of you create collaborative marketing strategies or share best practices for the good of the entire company?

FIGURE 8

With several would-be market thieves frozen in peculiar formations, the quick protector looks for new victims of his marketing plans.

Activity 9

Bucket of Pink Slips

I did exactly what you told me to do, that is why we failed. So who is responsible?

This activity can be a metaphor for coaching new employees, learning about active listening, taking responsibility for outcomes, or creating empathy for supervisors and subordinates during a role reversal. It all depends on who goes without sight and how you debrief the experience.

EQUIPMENT

- One small bucket filled with objects
- One slightly larger bucket that is empty
- Two 50-foot ropes tied in circles
- 8 blindfolds
- Stopwatch
- Flipchart
- Markers
- A small circle of Bungee cord with 8 ropes tied to it (each at least 10-feet long)

Remove all obstacles that a sightless person might run into or trip over.

Presentation

To set up for this activity, place one ground rope down in a giant circle.

In the very center of this circle, place the bucket filled with the objects.

Set the empty bucket in another giant rope circle ten feet away.

Place the Bungee loop three feet from the filled bucket inside the giant rope circle.

Spread the ropes attached to the Bungee loop out in a giant spider/sun beam/flower pattern so that at least one foot of each rope's end is outside of the ground rope circle.

The activity is set up so that each participant has a rope that connects him or her to the Bungee loop. If there are more participants than you have ropes, have the person holding the rope be sightless (eyes closed) and another person (their supervisor/manager) verbally instruct them - no touching each other! Only the sightless person may touch the ropes.

The bucket contains something awful to the group such as little backbiting remarks (office politics), layoffs, lost wages, unclosed sales, bad attitude employees, etc.,

If these were to spill onto the ground the company is adversely affected and the team is held accountable/responsible. If they are calling the objects 'layoffs', then for every object to fall out ten employees were laid off, and some of those employees must come from this team so do they want to try it again?

Safe handling of these issues means no objects dropped on the ground. Pouring all of the objects into the empty bucket and getting the original bucket back where it started from creates successful elimination of the problem or an effective prevention program. The basket in the

Technique Have the sightless rope holders create a list of attitudes, beliefs and behaviors that they expect from their coaches while the coaches go into the hall and use the Bungee contraption to see how it works. Then the sightless people are taken into the hall without ever seeing what the contraption looks like ahead of time.

layoff example would be a successfully planned reorganization or successfully developing new markets so that every employee in the organization remains vital and productive.

No one on the team may touch the ground rope or step inside of it. This would be 'crossing the lines'. Only the Bungee loop and ropes attached to it may touch the bucket or objects.

Successful completion of the activity looks like: the team gets the Bungee around the bucket near the top by pulling on the ropes to expand the loop and then lowering it around the bucket before letting it close. The bucket is carefully raised and taken to the other circle of rope. The bucket is tipped, and the objects pour out into the empty bucket without spilling. The now-empty bucket is taken back to its rope circle and set back down in the middle. This is not the only solution I have seen so do not punish the creative teams if they find a loophole in your presentation! Learn from it for next time.

Processing may focus on the roles that team members took, were they the same as back in the office? Who was a leader and why and what skills did they use that should be emulated in the office? Where did the most effective ideas come from and were all ideas heard or tried? Did the team give up on an idea too soon and is that reflective of the way ideas are treated at work? If pairs controlled the ropes, how effective was the communication? Did the blind subordinate team member seek clarification? Who was frustrated, why and how did it affect the team?

Debrief

These questions have proven to be very effective for many groups:

- Who in your organization feels sightless and frustrated? How can you go back and help them?

- Did the team have a shared goal that was understood by everyone? How did that affect the outcome?

- What coaching style proved to be most effective and why?

FIGURE 9

In this version, 'mentors' are helping their sightless 'protégés' make a mess of the ropes.

Hopefully, your team has more sense than to hopelessly twist the ropes.

Activity 10

Accidents, Incidents, and Near Misses

I meant what I said, but it was not what you heard.

Communication is the root of all evil in many otherwise healthy organizations. Everyone knows what he or she should be saying and how they should say it, but that does not make it any easier to actually behave in congruence with what we know works best. This activity is an opportunity to help leaders realize that their words have meaning, but not always the meaning they think they have.

EQUIPMENT

- Orange cones to mark a large rectangle on the ground
- Stopwatch
- Flipchart
- Markers
- One paper cup per participant
- One paper plate per participant
- One paper square per participant
- One pen per participant

Stand close to sightless people because they lose their balance very quickly in this activity. You have to catch them and steady them.

Presentation

Hand every participant at least one plate, cup and square to label with a marker or pen.

They are to write the name of a potential accident on the plate(s), the name of a potential incident on the cup(s), and the name of a potential near miss on the paper square(s). If they are not in manufacturing, you may have them label the items with three other types of avoidable problems. These might be a problem that leads to miscommunication (plates), a problem that leads to misunderstanding (cups), and a problem that leads to an assumption (squares). You may find that they list actual events from the office. That's okay because they will now have a chance to try to resolve those issues successfully.

Make a rectangle with the cones on the ground.

Each participant loudly calls out what he or she wrote on the paper products as each one is tossed into the rectangle on the floor. Repeat it if the team was not listening.

"Now we have a pit full of potential accidents, incidents and near misses. I believe that you will want to avoid coming into contact with these potential problems. In order to navigate your way through this month (motion to the rectangle), you will need a partner so please chose one now."

> **Technique** There is a sense of competition if you write the names of the partners on the flipchart and create a graph showing which pairs touched how many objects during their journeys through the month.

After they have a partner, "One of you will need to verbally guide the other through the month so that none of the problems are touched. Does anyone want to experience... (pick up one of the plates and read off of it). Well then how about only... (pick up a square and read off of it). The person being guided will need to rely heavily on their teammate because they will be blindfolded (or have their eyes closed). Which three pairs would like to go first? Please choose which person will be blindfolded first. The other partner will be blindfolded later." Often, the activity is done with partners on opposite sides of the rectangle, but they may want to move closer to their partner as long as they do not touch them. I usually have the first pairs go last after they switch so that they can learn from subsequent groups and be more successful. They will have learned to be more specific from the other pairs' experiences.

Have the three persons traversing the year close their eyes and turn in circles. Before they begin, move the items in the rectangle around randomly, but make sure that it is accomplishable. Ask them to begin. Repeat for each pairs' attempts.

Processing will focus on communication and following directions. Different personality types seek different types of communication. This would work well in conjunction with the Myers-Briggs as a clarifying activity. How do the different team members want to be supervised, instructed, led, or guided? What feedback do the givers of information desire? How do you know if the message is being perceived correctly? How should the office react to this new information? Write their ideas on the flipchart so that they make take them back and try them.

Debrief

Questions with impact:

- Who received excellent directions and what did those sound like? Do the leaders in your company always sound this way?
- Who wanted a different method of instructions and how did you ask for that? Can you ask people to explain things in a certain way at work?
- When are you this dependent on others for direction or success? How do you manage those situations?

FIGURE 10

Do you think he is peeking out of the bottom of his bandanna? That is why you should have them just close their eyes.

Activity 11

Office Politics

This is an effective way to allow the group to bring up some 'sticky situations' through a safe metaphor.

A creative facilitator told me about the time he filled a small treasure chest with little rocks for this activity. He put tiny bits of Velcro™ on every single little rock and used a chest that did not close well. When a participant latched onto the Velcro™ on the lid of the chest, all of the little rocks came pouring out! You see, tackling one large issue can often bring a flood of other smaller issues if you are not careful.

EQUIPMENT

- 10 strips of Velcro™ with a safety pin on one end and a fishing weight on the other (at least two to three feet long each)
- Markers
- An empty bucket
- Stopwatch
- Flipchart
- Balls and balloons with small Velcro™ squares taped or glued to them
- A can of spaghetti with Velcro™ taped around the outside
- A battery-operated toy that constantly moves with Velcro™ taped to its midsection

Prevent sexual harassment and offending comments by warning the group up front that they are unacceptable.

Presentation

Have the group chose a management team comprised of 20% of the participants. The management team may speak and touch the 'tails' of the staff and the bucket, but they may not touch the balls, balloons, etc. To increase the difficulty, do not allow the management team to touch the tails or bucket with their hands or arms. Ask the management team to have a brief planning meeting while you address the rest of the staff. The remainder of the participants will be 'staff' and must put on a 'tail'. Staff may not touch anyone's tail, including their own, and may not touch the balls, balloons, etc. The tail should be attached at the waistline of their pants with the safety pin. Belt loops work well.

> **Technique** Give different individual team members additional information such as a time limit or the fact that if the bucket falls over or is intentionally moved then the entire activity must start over. Observe their willingness or reluctance to share this information.

The items with the Velcro™ attached to them are placed on one side of the room/area and the bucket is placed on the other.

"Here is the scenario. These items represent the elements of office politics that can destroy the morale and efficacy of your employees. (Motion toward the balls, balloons, etc.) We have gossip and rumors (balls), kissing-up (balloons), the proverbial 'can of worms' (can of cheap pasta), and a nasty little power struggle (battery-operated toy or ball). The problems can be destroyed only if management and staff work together to eliminate their presence in the office. They may be eliminated fully only by placing every problem into the solution bucket. Therefore, the task is to get every item into the bucket. The only things that may touch the items are the tails. Sometimes problems just follow us around, but you have to be proactive in tackling them to eliminate them! You may begin." You may find that it works best to have one facilitator address the management team and tell them what they may do and what the objective is while the other facilitator addresses the staff. Then the management and staff must come together and discover what each may do and how to work together to accomplish the task.

Be very aware of sexual comments or issues. They must be eliminated immediately for this activity to work best.

Processing will focus on the relationship between management and staff, who the real leaders turned out to be, whether people had their needs met, ideas were heard or solutions were shared throughout the group. Metaphorical issues include who could handle which issues (fuzzy Velcro can not pick up other fuzzy Velcro), and how easily we can get seriously tangled in these politics when our intention is just to help resolve them (tails getting tangled).

Debrief

To open the post-activity discussion you might ask:

- How does your company really handle sticky situations?
- Which issues required the most effort and creativity to eliminate? Is that also true in the office?
- What worked here that might also work in your company?

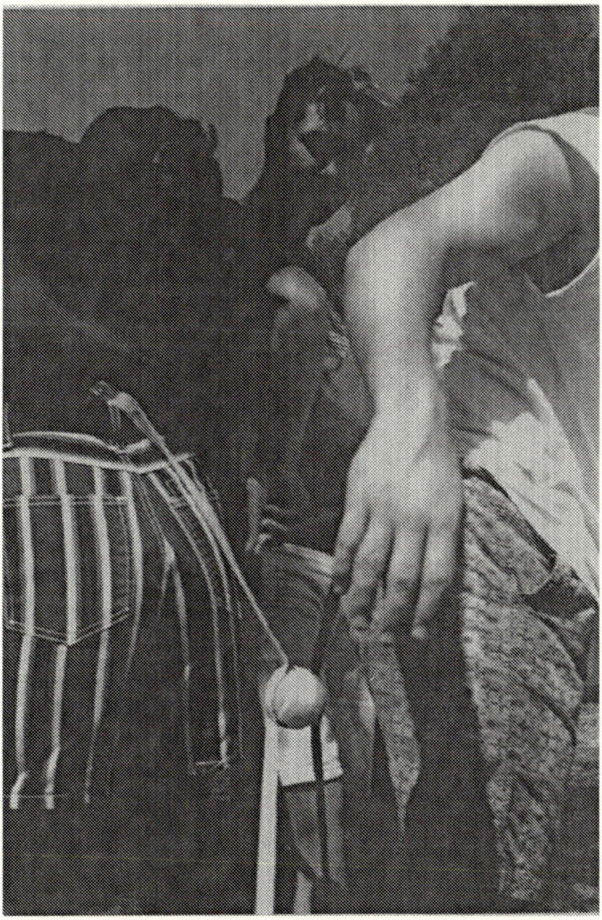

FIGURE 11

Tennis balls are heavier than they appear and require some collaborative efforts.

Activity 12

Closure

Meetings often end abruptly and no success is acknowledged or celebrated. Not anymore...

Too many companies forget to take the time to celebrate success. Only by recognizing and celebrating achievement can an organization hope to sustain and promote continued success.

EQUIPMENT

- Marketing supplies that double as prizes

Presentation

The facilitator or the company's highest-ranking official present at the meeting will offer a token to each participant one at a time in front of the whole team. This must have been pre-arranged with the client and may be logo-embossed T-shirts, caps, bandannas, etc., If the team is not too large, everyone may be able to sign each other's award with a permanent marker.

-OR-

The group is in a circle so that everyone can see and hear everyone else. Going around the circle, each person acknowledges to another member of the team something he or she appreciated about that person for the day and then they acknowledge themselves as well. You may wish to have the person who was appreciated go next until everyone has been acknowledged once by someone and once by themselves.

In the Brags version, team members randomly brag about the team, teammates and themselves

About the Author

Darin Phillips, PhD, CPT

Prior to starting www.darinphillips.com Darin managed the Learning and Performance team at Pennzoil-Quaker State (PQS) Company following its transformation from an oil company to a consumer products company. Darin is well known for his thorough design and creative solutions to organizational and team development needs.

In order to shift the culture at PQS and help ensure the needed transformation, the executive team developed a strategic Human Resources Plan. Darin helped to operationalize this plan by designing a comprehensive set of tools and processes that could be used throughout the company. These included team and organizational assessments (360s, behavioral interviewing tools, climate surveys); developmental solutions (instructor-led and self-paced training, coaching and mentoring assignments, work application assignments); and tracking tools (web-based appraisal and feedback forms, performance management system and toolbox). He was also responsible for hiring and training direct reports that could use and deliver these tools.

Previously Darin worked for small training and consulting firms and as a counselor. At Performa Solutions, Inc. Darin managed the development and deployment of 57 associate staff (trainers and consultants). This team delivered organizational and team developmental assessments and solutions for primarily Fortune 500 clients. Darin was the principal consultant on all critical engagements with key clients in the energy, retail, banking, hospitality, and management consulting fields.

Darin is the author of five books on group facilitation and teambuilding techniques, tips, and tools. He has also authored numerous trade publication articles on those topics, including his contribution to the McGraw-Hill 2000 Training and Performance Sourcebook.

Darin received his bachelor's degree in psychology from the University of Texas at Austin and his Ph.D. in psychology from Concordia. Darin is one of ISPI's original Certified Performance Technologists (CPT). Darin holds numerous certifications for type A and type B assessments including MBTI, FIRO-B, I-Opt, and the In-Q Thinking Inventory. Darin is also certified in many of the Lominger Leadership Architect tools.

<u>Also by Darin Phillips</u>

Facilitating Interpersonal Skills-Based Training Groups

http://www.darinphillips.com/products.htm

Twenty-eight activities and all of the questions necessary to create a great lesson plan for training, counseling, or teaching are rolled up into this classic book by Darin Phillips.

As an introduction to instructional design or as a classic reference book, this will find its way off of your shelf more than most of the resource or activity books that you may have collected over the years!

This classic text contains:

• the theoretical background for why these lesson plans work when teaching specific skills

• tons of questions to ensure that your create a program that meets the ergonomic, political, and educational needs of your participants

• warnings about the dangers of using music to warm up groups

• 11 fun and engaging Ice Breakers

• 4 effective closing activities

• a full 12-week group counseling agenda for angry 6th grade boys as an example + the keys to success when creating a lesson plan.

This text is perfect for teaching basic instructional design to subject matter experts (SME's) that are expected to teach a class, reminding teachers of the critical elements of a learning objective, learning several new activities to use in your training or counseling programs, and for completing an in-depth needs assessment. It is a quick and easy read filled with so many tips and tools that you will want to make sure your peers end up getting copies for themselves instead of constantly taking this one off of your desk.

For more information, see:

http://www.darinphillips.com/products.htm

Play, Play, Play: Games & Initiatives You Have Never Played Before Because I Just Made Them Up

http://www.darinphillips.com/products.htm

You really haven't seen these games before. This collection of activities created by one of the world's leading trainers and facilitators is chock full of fun and a few lessons about teamwork and problem solving.

Everyone should own a book that is 'dedicated to every child who builds forts out of blankets, especially while it is raining outside'. With activities such as All Tied Up, Hold the Anchovies, Elephant Trunks, and Shoot the Boss, this book is worth a look even if you will never train or facilitate a group during this lifetime.

For those people involved in teaching, training, consulting, youth groups, camps, meeting facilitation, ministry, and general group mayhem, this book is a welcome relief from the scores of activity guides that re-hash the same old material. This collection of 18 original activities will provide even the most experienced and well-read group leader with at least 16 exercises that no one in your group has ever seen before! (Just to be safe we say "16" because someone might have been in a previous group being led by one of the other owners of this book.)

Every activity is written in a concise format that covers the equipment required, guidelines for presentation, discussion topics for after the experience, and variations that may work better for your particular group.

Never hear these words again, "I have already done this activity..." At least not until you repeat these activities and all of their variations. That will take quite a while...

For more information, see:

http://www.darinphillips.com/products.htm

Printed in the United Kingdom
by Lightning Source UK Ltd.
123898UK00001B/91/A

9 781591 131700